D0579624

SANDY

DEVASTATION

AND

REBIRTH

AT THE

JERSEY SHORE

PROCEEDS

Portions of the proceeds will go to:

The Seaside Heights and Seaside Park volunteer fire departments

The Tri-Boro First Aid Squad, which provides service to communities affected by the 2013 fire

ON THE COVER:

Using a Canon 7D camera and 17-35 mm lens, and light-painting with flashlights during a five-minute time exposure, staff photographer Mark R. Sullivan created this final image of the Union Beach home that came to symbolize superstorm Sandy's destructive power. The house was demolished the next morning. PHOTO BY MARK R. SULLIVAN

ON THE BACK COVER:

An aerial view of the Seaside Park Boardwalk fire on the afternoon of September 12. PHOTO BY PETER ACKERMAN

ACKNOWLEDGEMENTS

THOMAS M. DONOVAN

President and Publisher, New Jersey Press Media

HOLLIS R. TOWNS

VP/News, New Jersey Press Media

JAMES FLACHSENHAAR

Managing Director, Content and Audience Development, New Jersey Press Media

JAMES J. CONNOLLY

Multimedia Editor, New Jersey Press Media

MAGDELINE BASSETT

Assistant Multimedia Editor, New Jersey Press Media

KAREN GUARASI

Regional VP/Advertising and Marketing, New Jersey Press Media

REGINA LONGO

Regional Marketing Manager, New Jersey Press Media

CHRIS MIHAL

Creative Director, New Jersey Press Media

Special thanks to:

Ann Hayes, Alyssa Calderone

Copyright © 2013 by Asbury Park Press

All Rights Reserved ISBN: 978-1-59725-478-6

No part of this book may be reproduced, stored in a retrieval system or transmitted in any form or by any means, electronic, mechanical, photocopying, recording or otherwise, without prior written permission of the copyright owner or the publisher.

Published by Pediment Publishing, a division of The pediment Group, Inc. www.pediment.com. Printed in Canada.

CONTENTS

A photograph of Elizabeth Spillane and her husband, discovered in the sand beneath their ruined Holgate home. PHOTO BY MARK R. SULLIVAN

On October 22, 2012,

Tropical Storm Sandy barely registered on New Jersey's radar as it developed in the western Caribbean. After all, we were slammed by Hurricane Irene only a year earlier. Could any storm be worse?

We didn't have to wait long for the answer. By October 29, Sandy was 900 miles wide. In satellite photos, it covered most of the East Coast. And by the time it struck New Jersey, its fury was enhanced by warm ocean waters and a snowstorm arriving from the west.

It wasn't pretty.

Sandy's 60-mph winds drove the Atlantic Ocean over sea walls and protective dunes.

The storm ripped apart piers and pushed trees through buildings.

It destroyed houses and businesses, washed away cars and boats, swept away protective dunes, flooded generating stations and splintered light poles.

The morning after Sandy slammed into New Jersey, 90 percent of the Shore was in the dark. Across the state, 2.5 million residents lost power.

Thousands of evacuees were stuck in shelters.

Hundreds of others were stranded in flooded houses, waiting for rescue.

Slowly, painfully, we made it through the first hours and days and weeks with an uncommon resolve. We stood in line for gasoline. We huddled for warmth. Mostly, we lent helping hands to family and friends, rediscovering in many cases the true meaning of community.

Yet less than a year later, on Thursday, September 12, 2013, a good part of the Seaside Park and Seaside Heights boardwalks went up in 25 mph wind-whipped flames. More than 60 businesses along five blocks were destroyed. Many of those businesses had just recovered from Sandy. Fortunately, there were no deaths or serious injuries from the fire.

We are pleased to present this second edition of "Sandy: Devastation and Rebirth at the Jersey Shore," complete with 24 pages of photos from the boardwalk blaze and an eerily similar 1955 fire.

Part of the profits from our Sandy books will be donated to the Seaside Heights and Seaside Park volunteer fire companies, and the Tri-Boro First Aid Squad.

THOMAS M. DONOVAN
PRESIDENT/PUBLISHER
NEW JERSEY PRESS MEDIA

PHOTO BY MARK R. SULLIVAN

CHAPTER 1

Calm before the storm

Fill up the car. Board the windows. Bring the televisions upstairs. Drop the pets at your sister's. We all know the drill. For some storms, preparation makes all the difference. And with superstorm Sandy churning up the coast, New Jerseyans were told to take every precaution.

But with no consensus on the storm's precise path, none of us were sure how damaging it would be. As the warnings grew, and Sandy's satellite image grew ever larger, we added hope to our preparation "to-do" list.

Finally, with the storm readying for a left-hand turn into the New Jersey coastline, most of us abandoned our homes to their fate. Only a few – either defiant or isolated – stayed behind to ride out Sandy's fury.

Oct. 29 — A curious resident stands at Old Bridgewater Front Park in Old Bridge, to watch as wind whips up the Raritan Bay with hurricane force winds. PHOTO BY MARK R. SULLIVAN

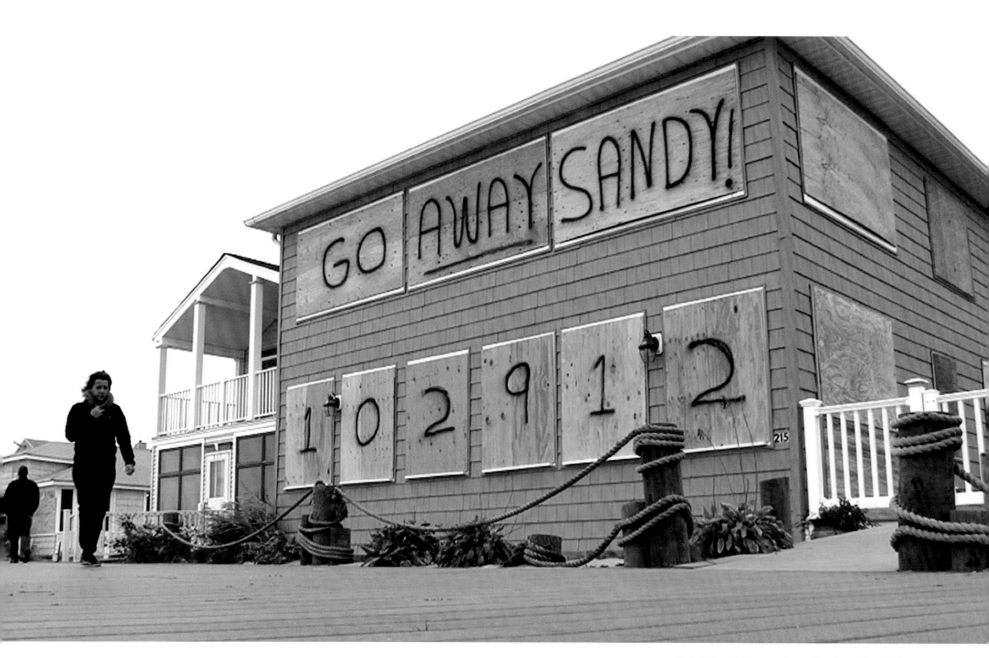

Oct. 28 — A home along the boardwalk in Point Pleasant Beach, has a message for superstorm Sandy. PHOTO BY THOMAS P. COSTELLO

Oct. 29 — A pedestrian in Morristown braces for superstorm Sandy. PHOTO BY BOB KARP

Oct. 29 — Top, in Denville, a business owner prepares his store for the storm.
PHOTO BY BOB KARP

Oct. 28 — Rough surf breaks over the Manasquan Inlet in Point Pleasant Beach ahead of superstorm Sandy. PHOTO BY THOMAS P. COSTELLO

A temporary shelter was established at Middlesex
County College, Edison Monday, November 5, 2012, in the
aftermath of superstorm Sandy. PHOTO BY JASON TOWLEN

Oct. 28 — Jack Frey, 14, hands a screw gun up to his father Chris as they board up the family's ocean front home on Broadway near the Manasquan Inlet in Point Pleasant Beach. Intense surf hit the Jersey Shore ahead of superstorm Sandy.
PHOTO BY THOMAS P. COSTELLO

Oct. 29 — Superstorm Sandy starts to show its effects in Perth Amboy. PHOTO BY AUGUSTO F. MENEZES

Oct. 28 — Ben Wright, 12, and his sister Samantha, 13, fill up sand bags at the end of Water Street at the boardwalk in Point Pleasant Beach, for neighbor Eric Seaberg.
PHOTO BY THOMAS P. COSTELLO

Oct. 28 — The only Post office in Sea Bright boarded up as Sandy approached. The town was devastated with heavy property loss and damage.

PHOTO BY MARY FRANK

Oct. 27 — Workers from Vision Construction Group in Edison build a wall of 20,000 sandbags around the PNC Bank at Newark Avenue and Route 35 North in Lavallette. PHOTO BY THOMAS P. COSTELLO

Oct. 29 — An emergency worker fills and stacks bags of sand in Perth Amboy.
PHOTO BY AUGUSTO F. MENEZES

Oct. 28 — Evacuation shelter was set up at the Brackman School in Barnegat and run by the Community Emergency Response Team.
PHOTO BY PETER ACKERMAN

Oct. 28 — Linda Walton, of Belford, owner of the Riverfront Restaurant in Sea Bright, carts away bags of sand in preparation for Sandy's landfall.
PHOTO BY MARY FRANK

Oct. 28 — Sandy Jenna Hetem, 15, of Atlantic Highlands, runs from the crashing waves on a jetty in Sea Bright, as superstorm Sandy began her assault. PHOTO BY MARY FRANK

Sandy strikes

O n the evening of Monday, October 29, 2012 the 900-mile wide behemoth – fueled by warm Atlantic Ocean waters and supercharged by a western snowstorm – crash-landed on the New Jersey coast near Atlantic City.

Although none of New Jersey was spared, Ocean and Monmouth counties bore the full brunt. Boardwalks went missing. Boats were smashed, sunk and tossed into houses. More than 2,500 light poles were snapped.

An unrelenting storm surge destroyed houses and businesses, buried cars, and damaged or destroyed the Shore's protective dunes. By the time the storm eased on Tuesday, thousands of us were swamped, thousands more homeless. So much for our carefully constructed defenses.

Nearly 3 million New Jerseyans lost power, many for more than two weeks. And in parts of some coastal communities, including Holgate, Ortley Beach, Lavallette, Mantoloking, Sea Bright, Union Beach, Point Pleasant and Seaside Heights, it wasn't clear when power – and people – would return.

Oct. 31 — Work crews clear sand from Route 35 in Ortley Beach. PHOTO BY DOUG HOOD

Oct 29 — Seaside Park is slammed by superstorm Sandy in these iPhone photos provided by Seaside Park Police Chief Francis Larkin.

Oct. 29 — From road to canal: Highlands is completely flooded by superstorm Sandy.

PHOTO BY TANYA BREEN

Oct. 31 — Houses still partially underwater in Belmar near Lake Como. PHOTO BY PETER ACKERMAN

Dec. 5 — Firefighters battle a fire in Manasquan.
PHOTO BY TOM SPADER

Oct. 30 — High tides forced boats out of their moorings and onto the shoreline of Cheesequake Creek in Old Bridge Twp. PHOTO BY MARK R. SULLIVAN

Nov. 29 — Large amounts of debris from superstorm Sandy washed up on the mainland next to the bay in the Forsythe National Wildlife Refuge in Brick. Brick Mayor Stephen Acropolis looks out over a massive debris field off St. Lawrence Blvd. in the township's Baywood section. PHOTO BY BOB BIELK

Oct. 30 — An uprooted tree closes a road in South River. PHOTO BY AUGUSTO F. MENEZES

Oct. 29 — Sparks fly after two downed primary wires made contact along Brick Boulevard, south of Drum Point Road, in Brick Township.

PHOTO BY THOMAS P. COSTELLO

Oct. 31 — **Fisherman's Pier in Keansburg, destroyed by superstorm Sandy.** PHOTO BY PETER ACKERMAN

Nov. 29 — The Jet Star roller coaster remains in the ocean in Seaside Heights. PHOTO BY TANYA BREEN

Oct. 31 — Pilings in the sand are all that remained of Lisa and Dan O'Hara's East Avenue home in Bay Head. PHOTO BY THOMAS P. COSTELLO

Nov. 18 — A helicopter carrying Vice President Joe Biden tours the Jersey shore to evaluate damage from supertsorm Sandy. The chopper is flying over the Belmar beachfront. PHOTO BY THOMAS P. COSTELLO

Nov.29 — Aerial view of Mantoloking, where the
ocean cut an inlet to the bay. STAFF PHOTO TANYA BREEN

Nov. 15 — The remains of a burned-out Camp
Osborn home along Route 35 north in the barrier
island section of Brick Township. The area was
destroyed by fires following superstorm Sandy.
PHOTO BY THOMAS P. COSTELLO

Dec. 18 — NJ DOT commissioner James Simpson surveys the damage to Ortley Beach.
PHOTO BY BOB BIELK

Nov. 24 — A miniature golf course located along the Point Pleasant Beach boardwalk was leveled by the surge during superstorm Sandy.
PHOTO BY MARK R. SULLIVAN

Nov. 29 — Aerial view of repairs at the Mantoloking Bridge, where the ocean cut an inlet to the bay. PHOTO BY TANYA BREEN

Oct. 29 & 31 — In these before-and-after images, Lisa and Dan O'Hara's East Avenue, Bay Head home is assaulted by a flood surge that washed over the dunes, left. All that was left of the home after Sandy were pilings in the sand.

PHOTOS BY THOMAS P. COSTELLO

Nov. 18 — Joey Harrison's Surf Club in Ortley Beach (far left) was leveled by superstorm Sandy. PHOTO BY THOMAS P. COSTELLO

Nov. 14 — The Asbury Park boardwalk after Sandy came ashore. PHOTO BY MARY FRANK

Dec. 27 — Washington Avenue in Rumson is flooded again after a winter storm brought more rain to the superstorm-ravaged town. PHOTO BY MARY FRANK

Oct. 31 — At right, arcade games, bumper cars and game prizes riddle Beachway in the Keansburg Amusement Park. PHOTO BY TANYA BREEN

Oct. 31 — A large section on the roof of the Great Auditorium in Ocean Grove was ripped off by the winds of superstorm Sandy. PHOTO BY PETER ACKERMAN

Oct. 31 — Camp Osborne in Brick Twp. still smolders, days after superstorm Sandy hit the area. PHOTO BY PETER T. ACKERMAN

Oct. 30 — Flooding and damage in South River.
PHOTO BY AUGUSTO F. MENEZES

Nov. 8 — Cars make their way around a fallen tree along Herbertsville Road in Wall Twp. An overnight Nor'easter brought high winds and snow, up to 12 inches in some places, to New Jersey.
PHOTO BY MARK R. SULLIVAN

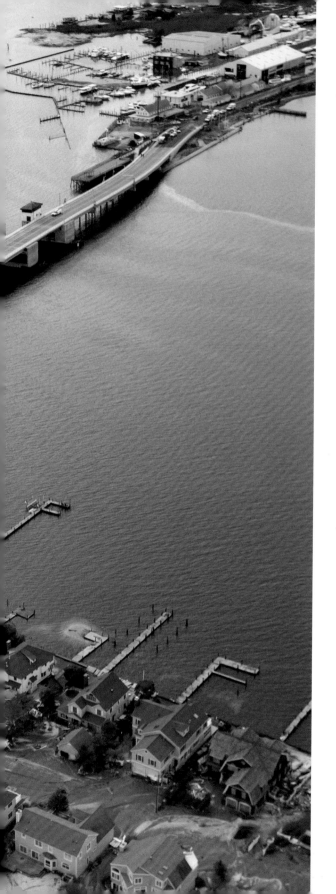

Oct.31 — At left, Bridge to nowhere: The Mantoloking Bridge after Sandy washed out its Eastern landing. PHOTO BY PETER ACKERMAN

Nov. 8 — Damaged houses along Ocean Avenue in Ortley Beach at dusk. PHOTO BY THOMAS P. COSTELLO

CHAPTER 3

Chaos and suffering

S andy claimed the lives of more than three dozen New Jerseyans, including five in Monmouth and Ocean counties.

Its other victims endured days of waiting – for gasoline, a hot shower and, for many still stuck in shelters, the opportunity to return home. For the unluckiest, those homes were either uninhabitable or swept away by the storm surge.

In many ways, waiting for electricity to be restored caused the most frustration, and not only because it powers our appliances, our quality of life, and our connection to the world. Simply not knowing when the lights would come back on caused tempers to fray and put utilities under the microscope.

Officials prevented residents from returning to storm-ravaged areas until services could be restored. In some cases it would be months before they were allowed to permanently return. And when they did, they found neighborhoods that were irrevocably changed.

Nov. 20 — Anna Yurgelonis, a resident of Brook Avenue in Union Beach, tries to pick up the pieces of her life after her home was destroyed during superstorm Sandy. She offers comfort to her grandchild, Jaelyn Yurgalonis, 7, who lived in the home with her. PHOTO BY MARY FRANK

Oct. 30 — At right, a resident looks over the aftermath of a house explosion along Noe Street in Carteret that burned three homes to the ground. The family in the residence had just been rescued by rising floodwaters from superstorm Sandy.
PHOTO BY MARK R. SULLIVAN

Nov. 11 — Above, Ken Barran, 75, of Virginia Drive, Stafford Twp., surveys his damaged home. His boat "Sparky" sits across the lagoon on the back deck of one of his neighbors. PHOTO PETER ACKERMAN

Nov. 7 — At left, Governor Chris Christie takes questions at the High Point Fire Company in Harvey Cedars on Long Beach Island. He was there ahead of a Nor'easter that struck the Jersey Shore.

PHOTO BY THOMAS P. COSTELLO

Nov. 7 — Governor Christie pauses during the press conference in Harvey Cedars.

PHOTO BY THOMAS P. COSTELLO

Nov. 1 — At left, Devastation on Brook Avenue in Union Beach. PHOTOS BY TANYA BREEN

Nov. 7 — Michelle Miller of Morristown braces against wind and snow as she and her 3-year-old son, Mahlon, walk on South Street as a Nor'easter approaches. PHOTO BY BOB KARP

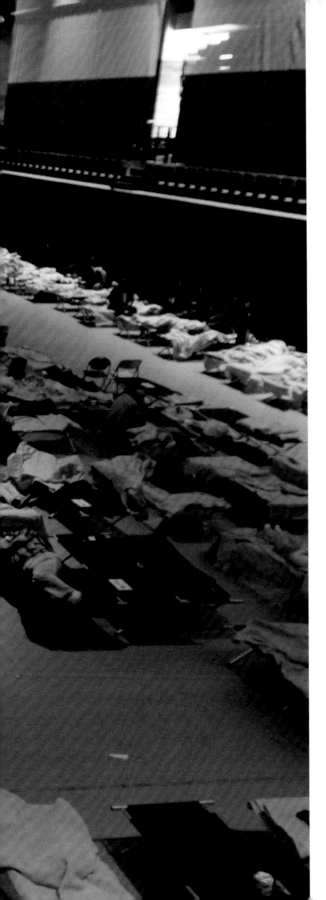

Oct. 31 — At left, cots fill the floor at in West Long Branch at Monmouth University's MAC gym. This was one of Monmouth County's shelters in the wake of superstorm Sandy. PHOTO BY THOMAS P. COSTELLO

Nov. 4 — Shirley Smith of Morristown helps herself to breakfast served at St. Peter's Episcopal Church. The church served three meals a day to those affected by superstorm Sandy.

PHOTO BY BOB KARP

Nov. 1 — At right, Jack and Colleen Feeney of 725 Brook Avenue in Union Beach sit on the front steps of what was their home, which was destroyed during Sandy. PHOTO BY TANYA BREEN

ANGELS GATHER HERE

Nov. 1 — Scenes of devastation on Brook Avenue in Union Beach. PHOTOS BY TANYA BREEN

Nov. 1 — At left, the Front Street, Union Beach home sheared in half by Sandy became an iconic image of the superstorm's destruction. PHOTOS BY TANYA BREEN

Nov. 8 — Carolyn Gursky of Pine Street in Union Beach surveys her home as volunteers from Christian Aid Ministries break apart her flooded walls and floors. PHOTO BY TANYA BREEN

Nov. 25 — At right, former Sayreville firefighter Jennifer Awad and friends Wendy and Bob Barbely organized a surprise fundraiser for George Gawron, first assistant fire chief, who lost his home in the flooding from superstorm Sandy. The fundraising breakfast took place at Carasso's Luncheonette in Milltown. PHOTO BY AUGUSTO F. MENEZES

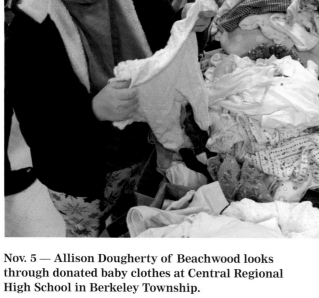

Nov. 5 — Allison Dougherty of Beachwood looks through donated baby clothes at Central Regional High School in Berkeley Township.
PHOTO BY THOMAS P. COSTELLO

Oct. 31 — Cars queue for gasoline along the Garden State Parkway service area in Wall Twp. PHOTO BY MARY FRANK

Nov. 2 — Ray Scribner of Paradise Park, a mobile home community in Highlands, returns to his devastated trailer to search for personal belongings. His cat, Tan, was found safe.

STAFF PHOTO TANYA BREEN

Nov. 1 — Muriel Lauer, left, and Agnela Spruiel,
both forced from their Keyport homes, took refuge
in a temporary shelter at Keyport Central School.
PHOTO BY TANYA BREEN

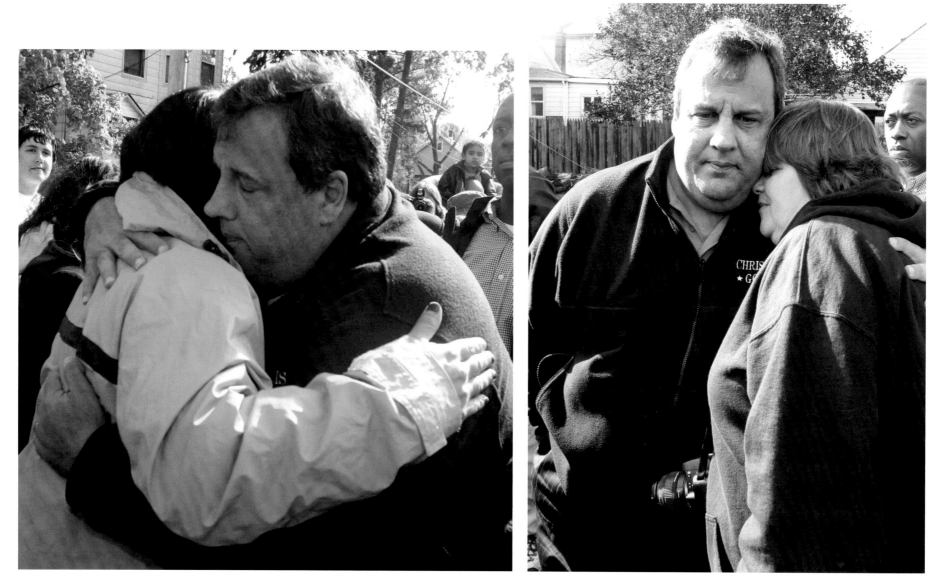

Oct. 31 — Gov. Chris Christie consoles Sharon Kloc,
left, and Carolyn McNutt, both of Sayreville, as he
toured the devastated community.

PHOTO BY MARK R. SULLIVAN

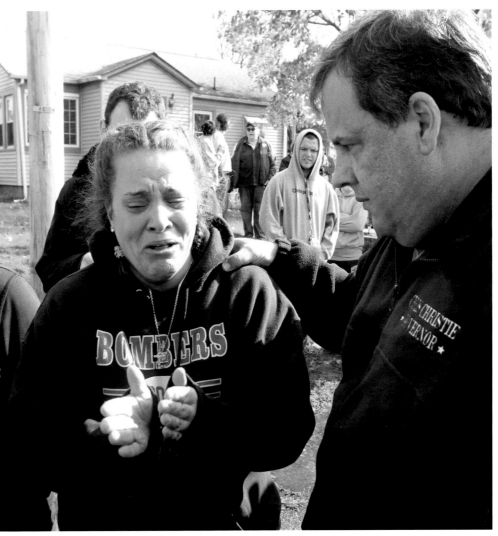

Oct. 31 — During a visit to hard-hit Sayreville, Gov. Christie told neighborhood children that Halloween would be postponed, top left, and also connected with residents Jean Churro, above left, and another William Street resident.

PHOTO BY MARK R. SULLIVAN

Nov. 6 — At right, Michael McDonald of Union Beach stands in the kitchen of his Brook Avenue home. McDonald escaped wearing his wet suit and riding his boogie board through the window of his dining room. PHOTO BY TANYA BREEN

Nov. 9 — Laurie Molinaro, a year-round Seaside Heights resident, returns to collect necessities. Residents had just 4 hours to gather items.
PHOTO BY TANYA BREEN

Nov. 9 — At left, Seaside Heights landlord Toni Giordano hugs her tenant, Colleen Kamil, as she tearfully surveys her Blaine Avenue property for the first time since the storm. PHOTO BY TANYA BREEN

Nov. 9 — Property owners and residents wait for instruction after arriving to Seaside Heights to assess damage and collect personal items from their damaged homes. PHOTO BY TANYA BREEN

Oct. 30 — Powerless, two Manville rooming house residents use an outdoor fire to keep warm and make a pot of morning coffee. PHOTO BY KATHY JOHNSON

**Oct. 31 — Motorists wait along Abbett Avenue
in Morristown to purchase gasoline
in the aftermath of superstorm Sandy.**

PHOTO BY BOB KARP

Dec. 11 — At right, the supports of a raised
Tuckerton house are used as a makeshift
drying rack. PHOTO BY PETER ACKERMAN

Nov. 2 — Loretta Dibble of Paradise Park, a mobile
home community in Highlands, returns to her
devastated trailer to search for personal belongings.
PHOTO BY TANYA BREEN

CHAPTER 4

Rebirth and hope

It started slowly. A road cleared here. A utility pole repaired there. Shorter lines for gas, blankets and water. A school returning to normal schedule.

Volunteers by the hundreds and thousands, many from out of state, joined the recovery effort. They cleared debris, comforted the elderly, and raised money and hope. At "12-12-12, The Concert for Sandy Relief," New Jersey's favorite son, Bruce Springsteen, channeled the resilience already resurgent among Sandy victims:

"My home's here on the Jersey Shore

"Come on and take your best shot

"Let me see what you've got

"Bring on your wrecking ball"

We are still recovering from Sandy, many of us awash in red tape and unexpected expenses. Did the superstorm force us to reexamine what it means to live at the Shore? Yes. Will other storms follow? Of course.

But if the energy and emotion of our shared recovery is any indication, we'll be right here to meet them.

Nov. 4 — Parishioners unite for Mass at the Church of St. Rose, Belmar in the aftermath of superstorm Sandy. PHOTO BY JASON TOWLEN

Nov. 19 — At left, Sheena Stevens of Union Beach hugs her 6-year-old daughter, Lateria Stevens, as she lines up for her first day at Saint Catherine's School, the temporary school for Union Beach Memorial School students. PHOTO BY TANYA BREEN

Nov. 25 — Alison Evans-Fragale of Atlantic Highlands cheers during The Hope for Highlands Concert, an event to raise funds for superstorm Sandy rebuilding efforts. PHOTO BY MARY FRANK

Nov. 3 — At right, workers from the Monmouth County, Department of Public Works begin the task of clearing sand and debris in Spring Lake.

PHOTO BY MARK R. SULLIVAN

Nov. 5 — Karen Pethybridge sorts through belongings at the curb outside her Surf City home.

PHOTO BY PETER ACKERMAN

Nov. 4 — At left, 15-month-old Za'Inah Tolliver of Morristown gets a comforting hug from volunteer Caitlin Lynch of Randolph during breakfast at St Peter's Episcopal Church in Morristown.
PHOTO BY BOB KARP

Dec. 1 — Volunteers from Woodhaven Lumber and Millwork distribute cleaning supplies, shovels, and diapers in Seaside Heights. PHOTO BY DOUG HOOD

Jan. 9 — A crowd gathers around Governor Chris Christie and Belmar Mayor Matt Doherty as the first boardwalk piling is driven on the beach in Belmar. PHOTO BY MARY FRANK

Dec. 18 — Bulldozers create a huge dune in Ortley Beach, in front of an area that sustained massive damage in superstorm Sandy. PHOTO BY BOB BIELK

Dec. 21 — The Union Beach house that became a symbol for devastation by superstorm Sandy is razed by volunteers. PHOTO BY PETER ACKERMAN

Nov. 4 — At left, Belmar first responders bow their heads in prayer during Sunday Mass at the Church of St. Rose, Belmar. PHOTO BY JASON TOWLEN

Nov. 4 — Parishioners gather for Mass at the Church of St. Rose. PHOTO BY JASON TOWLEN

Dec. 5 — "Train" performs at the Sea Bright
firehouse to entertain and benefit first responders.
PHOTO BY AUGUSTO F. MENEZES

Dec. 11 — At right, Victoria Mackies helps to clean
the storage garage at Stan's Marina in Waretown.
PHOTO BY PETER ACKERMAN

Nov. 4 — A sign outside Janine Miller's
Philadelphia Avenue house in Point Pleasant
summed up the resiliency of Sandy storm victims.
PHOTO BY THOMAS P. COSTELLO

Nov. 21 — At left, Rebecca O'Neill of Union Beach, who lost her Prospect Avenue home, rocks her 16-month-old daughter, Keira, to sleep in her family's temporary West Keansburg residence.

PHOTO BY TANYA BREEN

Dec. 20 — Even Santa Claus spoke to Gov. Chris Christie during a town hall meeting in Belmar.

PHOTO BY DOUG HOOD

Nov. 6 — Bob Englander of Morristown votes with his sons Holt, (5) and Karsten (9) in Town Hall in Morristown on Election Day. PHOTO BY BOB KARP

Nov. 6 — Voters make their way to voting machines
set up at Pinelands Regional High School.

PHOTO BY PETER ACKERMAN

Feb. 5 — At right, crew level the sand to begin rebuilding the Seaside Heights boardwalk.
PHOTO BY MARK R. SULLIVAN

Nov. 8 — Carolyn Gursky of Union Beach examines family photographs drying in a room above her **garage.** PHOTO TANYA BREEN

Nov. 9 — At left, the Spring Lake boardwalk looking north from the pool pavilion.
PHOTO BY THOMAS P. COSTELLO

Dec. 1 — New York Giants players visit the Lake Riviera Middle School, Brick and distribute gifts donated by Walmart. PHOTO BY BOB WARD

Nov. 10 — At right, Alene Stewart, a parent of an alumni, carries a cross from Saint Rose High School in Belmar into storage while clean up and repairs continue at the school. PHOTO BY TOM SPADER

Feb. 5 — A sign planted near the foundation of a destroyed Union Beach home, announces the owner's intention to rebuild.
PHOTO BY THOMAS P. COSTELLO

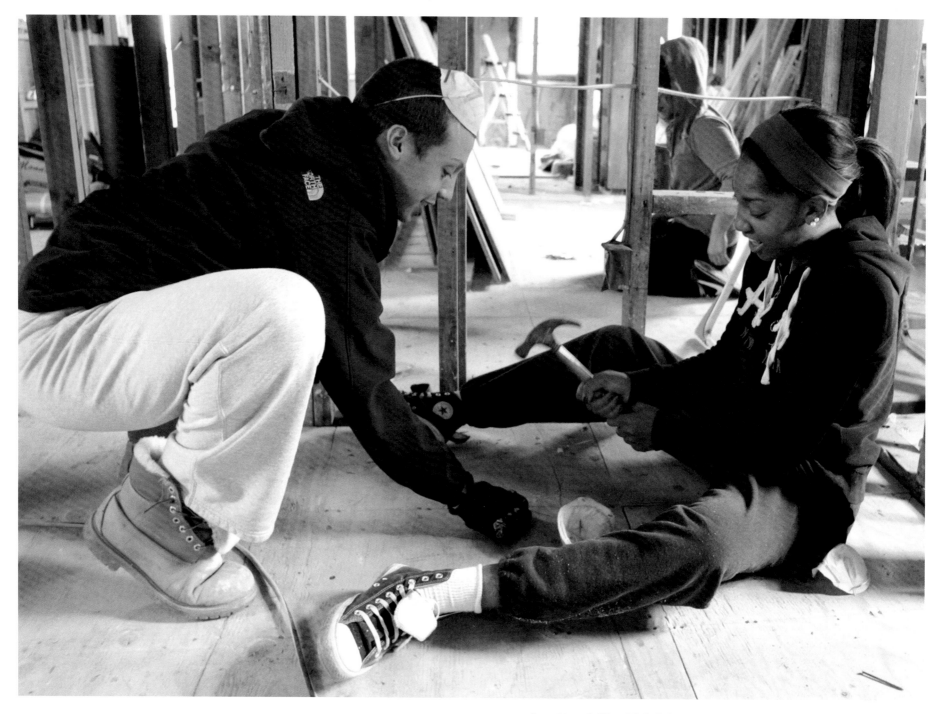

Jan. 29 — Collier High School student Richard Rizzieri, 17, of Neptune, left, steadies a nail while fellow student Midori Taylor, 16, of Ewing, hammers it into the flooring. They were helping to rebuild the home of fellow student Julia Christiano in Union Beach. PHOTO BY MARY FRANK

Nov. 3 — About 1,000 volunteers showed up to clean
up the Sadowski Parkway in Perth Amboy.

PHOTO BY AUGUSTO F. MENEZES

At left, Residents of Weber Avenue, Sayreville, gather in their powerless neighborhood.

Nov. 4 — Cindy Cama of Belmar, center, and Bea Dunn of Shark River Hills, right, are among the parishioners at Sunday Mass at the Church of St. Rose, Belmar. PHOTO BY JASON TOWLEN

Feb. 16 — At left, dawn find the beginning of the rebuilding of the Seaside Heights Boardwalk. The work would continue at a rate of 65 pilings per day.
PHOTO BY MARK R SULLIVAN

Nov. 9 — A sign outside Fantasy Island Amusement Park in Beach Haven welcomes a new summer season. PHOTO BY MARK R. SULLIVAN

CHAPTER 5

Voices of Sandy

I n many ways, the story of superstorm Sandy can be authentically told only by its victims – our neighbors who lost homes, possessions, peace of mind and even their love of life on the ocean.

From restaurateurs struggling to re-open, to a couple who watched their neighborhood burn down around them, to a 9-year-old member of her school's safety guard, these are the voices of Sandy — in a study in black and white.

Keansburg Amusement Park, like most bayshore businesses, suffered mightily from the wind and waves of Superstorm Sandy. Its owners, however, embrace the challenge as a chance to not only rebuild but add improvements along the way.
PHOTOS BY PETE ACKERMAN

Barbara DeJessa

Brick mother and daughter pull through

OCEAN GROVE — Barbara DeJessa's voice is strong and limned with laughter. But the strain of the past several weeks is there, too.

When the storm wrecked her two-bedroom rented bungalow in Brick, it also upended the daily routine and network of services she'd carefully constructed for her 12-year-old daughter, Helena Gross, who has a rare genetic condition that limits her speech.

They are attached at the hip, these two. For now, mother and daughter are sharing a suite at the Majestic Hotel, a pretty bed-and-breakfast near the beach in Ocean Grove, for as long as their temporary rental assistance holds out. Their landlord is rebuilding their bungalow, but there's no telling when they'll be back.

"I worry because I'm a mom, and I have a daughter who needs a whole lot, and I'd hate to have to uproot her," said DeJessa, 52. "Me, I know I'm a survivor. I've always been a survivor. I lost a brother in Vietnam. My father died when I was young. I was on my own when I was very young, and I'll be a survivor forever. So I know some way, somehow, I'll pull through and we'll work it out."

— **Shannon Mullen**

John J. Lederer Jr.

Architect strives to return beauty to ravaged town

BAY HEAD — On warm, summer days, people love to stroll along East Avenue — a narrow, north-to-south one-way thoroughfare that hugs the beachfront for a couple of miles without ever losing the aura of a private lane — and ogle the grand, cedar-shingled homes on either side of the street, drinking in their big, breezy porches, dormered windows and fragrant rose gardens.

"This," you can almost hear them say, "is the life."

Superstorm Sandy has turned those sighs into groans. In parts of Bay Head and throughout neighboring Mantoloking, the damage is jaw-dropping. Scores of homes, or what's left of them, are twisted into painful contortions. Some have fallen face first into the sand, like toddlers upended by the surf. Others simply have disappeared, leaving behind disorienting stretches of bare, shadowless dunes.

For many storm survivors, the rebuilding process will begin with a call to Bay Head architect John J. Lederer Jr. Over the years, he's designed some of the area's most beautiful homes — small, medium and hedge-fund sized. Now, in the latter stage of his career, he's facing what is perhaps his greatest professional challenge.

Complicating the task is the uncertainty about what the building regulations will be. "We're all running around in a fog, so to speak," he said.

"We need to get the rules straightened out, and they need to be common sense-oriented rules that people can afford ... rather than some knee-jerk reaction to what happened," Lederer said.

"It will get sorted out. I think these things will evolve and the rules will become clearer, but it's going to take time to do that. Not just six months," he said, "but years."

— Shannon Mullen

Mike Boeckel

Recovering from Sandy is a family affair

LAVALLETTE — For Mike Boeckel, the two weeks he spent in Lavallette every summer as a kid were the most fun — and fastest — 14 days of the year.

What he and his six siblings wouldn't have given to stretch those family vacations just a little bit longer, like a piece of salt water taffy pulled to the absolute limits permitted by the laws of physics.

So imagine what it meant when Mike, a construction worker, and his wife, Antonietta, a title agent, who live in East Hanover, were able to buy a piece of property in Lavallette that had not one but two beach bungalows on the same lot. It was a tight squeeze, but between the two houses there was enough room to fit the large contingent of relatives and friends who have enjoyed the arrangement just as much as the Boeckels and their two children, Nicolina, 14, and Michael, 12.

On a typical summer weekend, Mike said, "you'd see tables and chairs and people all over, and my wife on the beach until 6."

Thanks to Sandy, Mike's weekends are now spent repairing both houses, which were badly damaged in the storm. It's a tough situation, to be sure, but Mike, 47, and his chief helpers — his son, brother Steve, and brother-in-law, Mario Macero — make the most of their time together. To see them joking around and hear Mike's booming laugh, you'd think it was the Fourth of July.

— **Shannon Mullen**

Richard Domaratius

'I never really thought I was going to die'

BRICK — Richard Domaratius stood in the midst of the firestorm and watched Camp Osborn burn to the ground.

"It was like a blizzard of embers. Instead of it being white, it was all red," said Domaratius, 65. "I can remember the smell of smoke, the sound of ruptured gas lines and embers hitting me in the face. It was just terrible. Total devastation."

Camp Obsorn, a 60-unit bungalow community located near the southern end of Brick Township's portion of the barrier island, was destroyed after a fast-moving fire during the storm.

"People ask all of the time if I was scared. I guess I was, but I was more in survival mode," said Domaratius. "I was trying to keep my house from burning down, keep my wife and myself alive. I never really thought I was going to die."

During the fire, which burned from 9 p.m. to 5 a.m., Domaratius kept police informed about the fire until his cellphone died at around 11 p.m. At the height of the storm, local fire departments were unable to access Camp Osborn because of the rising floodwaters, police said.

"We honestly believed that our house was going to go up," Domaratius said. "The only thing that saved us was the wind shifting."

— **Nicholas Huba**

William Gelhaus

'We're making it better'

KEANSBURG — First impressions can be misleading.

Right after the storm, for example, the Keansburg Amusement Park was a shambles. The Wildcat roller coaster was inundated with five feet of sand. Bumper cars were scattered through town. The carousel looked like a goner.

The century-old amusement park seemed to have about as much life left in it as the unblinking, drowned Bart Simpson doll that was left lying on side on the ground beside one of the battered arcades.

Yet, despite an estimated $2 million in storm damage, William Gelhaus, the park's co-owner, says he fully expects the repairs and a previously planned $1 million upgrade to the Runaway Rapids Waterpark to be completed this spring.

"It's a little like putting Humpty Dumpty back together again, but that's what we do," Gelhaus said. "Everything we touch, we're making it better."

— **Shannon Mullen**

Joan DeLucia

Brooklyn attitude drives woman's quest to clean up

TOMS RIVER — The accent — and attitude — is pure Brooklyn.

Joan DeLucia, now of Toms River, isn't the type to back down from a fight.

Seeing the mess that superstorm Sandy left in her community so annoyed her (although "annoyed" is not how she phrases it) that she's spent the past two months marshaling large groups of volunteers to muck out scores of flooded homes in Ortley Beach and other hard-hit sections of the township.

DeLucia, 53, calls her Facebook-driven campaign Sandy Weekday Warriors — "weekday" because she says the needs are so great, sending cleanup crews out on weekends alone isn't enough.

This past Monday, the Martin Luther King Jr. Day holiday, DeLucia again had about 160 people out there working, this time on Pelican Island. She says she targeted that area, just west of the Thomas A. Mathis Bridge, because seeing all the debris strewn in the marsh there really, you know, irked her.

Another thing that … sets her off is seeing people with cameras, merrily snapping photos of the destruction.

"I go up to them and say, 'Are you here to volunteer?' And when they say, 'No, I'm not here to volunteer,' " I say, "Oh? What would you be doing here then?'"

"It's like a graveyard," DeLucia said, her Brooklyn sensibilities simmering again.

"People's lives are in that sand."

— **Shannon Mullen**

Scott and Carolyn Edrington

A life away from their beach

ORTLEY BEACH — Many of the major moments in Scott Edrington's life happened on the sands and in the surf of Ortley Beach.

It was there that he learned how to surf, and where he worked one of his first jobs, as a bus boy at the Surf Club. And it was there that he married his long-time girlfriend, Carolyn Wulff, on the deck of the beach house his grandfather built in 1954.

He and Carolyn, now 54, had met on the beach when he was working as a lifeguard back in 1981.

With superstorm Sandy bearing down on the Jersey Shore, the Edringtons fled, grabbing some important papers, a few clothes and their tabby cat, Sushi.

"I told people to go," Scott, 58, said. "Even if you survive it, you're going to be miserable for many, many hours."

That night, the storm's surge breached Ortley's dune line, destroying the house and upending the Edringtons' lives.

He lost more than a dozen of his prized long boards, although he's recovered seven of them since the storm.

Now living at a house in Berkeley's Bayville section, the Edringtons miss their house by the sea.

The way the light looks is different inland, and the sounds aren't the same.

"You wake up and it's different," he said of living in Bayville. "You don't see the ocean. You don't smell it."

— **Jean Mikle**

Kathy Barisciano

'We're heartbroken for our neighborhood'

ORTLEY BEACH — A look out the window of Kathy Barisciano's Ortley Beach dream home reveals the disaster superstorm Sandy wrought on the barrier beach community.

A piece of gray-shingled roof, pink shards of insulation and splintered strands of brown wood are smashed against the rear of the Nichols Avenue house she shares with her partner, Cindy Pagano, 62. A backyard full of debris is all that's left of three of her neighbors' homes.

"Never in my wildest dreams would I have imagined this kind of destruction," said a resigned but resolute Barisciano, 55. "We're heartbroken for our neighborhood."

Only seven months ago, they moved into the house, which replaced a small bungalow on the property that Barisciano had owned for 17 years.

Barisciano and Pagano have already gutted the first floor of their home, where water rose to the top of the stove, buckling the wood flooring and leaving behind more than an inch of slimy brown muck.

"There is something leaning on the back of my house and I can't fix my house," Barisciano said. "This is unprecedented, really. When you have houses on other people's houses, and on other people's property, it's still just hard to believe."

— **Jean Mikle**

Amanda Lewis

'Now we're back, and everybody's happy'

BAY HEAD — As a member of the safety patrol at Bay Head School, Amanda Lewis, 9, wears her belt and badge with pride.

Amanda takes her duties seriously. When the younger kids get lost in the hallway, she steers them in the right direction. If a boy is running too fast on the sidewalk, she'll slow him down before he gets hurt.

Even the best safety patrol officer in the world, however, could not protect the 112-year-old Bay Head School from superstorm Sandy. The flood damage to the building's lower level was so severe, Amanda and her schoolmates had to attend an elementary school in nearby Point Pleasant Beach for four weeks until it was safe for them to return.

On their first day back, Amanda was there to greet them at the front door.

"Now we're back, and everybody's happy," she said.

— **Shannon Mullen**

Karen and Daniel Picard

Losing everything and starting over

POINT PLEASANT BEACH — Before the storm, Karen and Daniel Picard were the busy owners of two successful restaurants on the same street in Point Pleasant Beach.

Both businesses are empty shells right now.

Talk about climate change.

There are at least 450,000 reasons for the Picards, whose home in the borough was also damaged, to feel utterly forlorn. That's the dollar amount they estimate they lost at Daniel's Bistro and Daniel's Trattoria.

The couple assumed their insurance would cover a catastrophe like this. Their insurance company has told them otherwise.

So what now?

If you're the Picards, you start over. They've opened a new place, Daniel's Bistro by the Sea (danielsbistronj.com) in a little storefront at 526 Main St. in Avon.

"We're back to a very small restaurant; we only seat 40," Karen Picard said. "But we have to move on."

— **Shannon Mullen**

CHAPTER 6

How you saw it

W e boarded up our homes, waited in line for gas, made sure loved ones were safe and sound – and we also took pictures … lots of pictures. If our first reaction to Sandy's devastation was grief, the second was an iron resolve to rebuild. For many, that began with documenting the extent of our losses so that, soon, we would see how far we had come.

Taken from a kite-mounted camera, an aerial shot of Belmar. SUBMITTED BY TOM LOZINSKI

Oct. 30 — A scene in the Bayville section of Berkeley Township the morning after Sandy struck. SUBMITTED BY DOUGLAS BENCE

Oct. 30 — Rick Pullen, chief diver with the Berkeley Township Underwater Search and Rescue Unit, helps residents to safety.
SUBMITTED BY DOUGLAS BENCE

Oct. 30 — Flung together by the superstorm, boats line the shore in Middletown.
SUBMITTED BY SONIA SZCZESNA

Oct. 29 — Superstorm Sandy approaches in Long Branch. UNKNOWN

Oct. 29 — Waves break against a house in Little Silver. This photo was taken at 8:40 p.m., about two hours before high tide. SUBMITTED BY BILL WETZEL

A series of images taken with a kite-mounted camera by Tom Lozinski in the weeks following Sandy. Below, Belmar. SUBMITTED BY TOM LOZINSKI

The Belmar beach.

Sea Girt.

Manasquan.

A tree crashed into a Monmouth Parkway house in Monmouth Beach
SUBMITTED BY TORI MAURO

A scene repeated across the path of Sandy: A dark house, a demand for power.
UNKOWN

Seaside Heights Boardwalk.
UNKNOWN

Sandy jumbled the natural order of things, like re-locating this boat to a Berkeley Township backyard.
SUBMITTED BY DOUGLAS BENCE

Defeated but still standing, a home on Bayshore
Drive in Barnegat. SUBMITTED BY NORMAN RUSSO

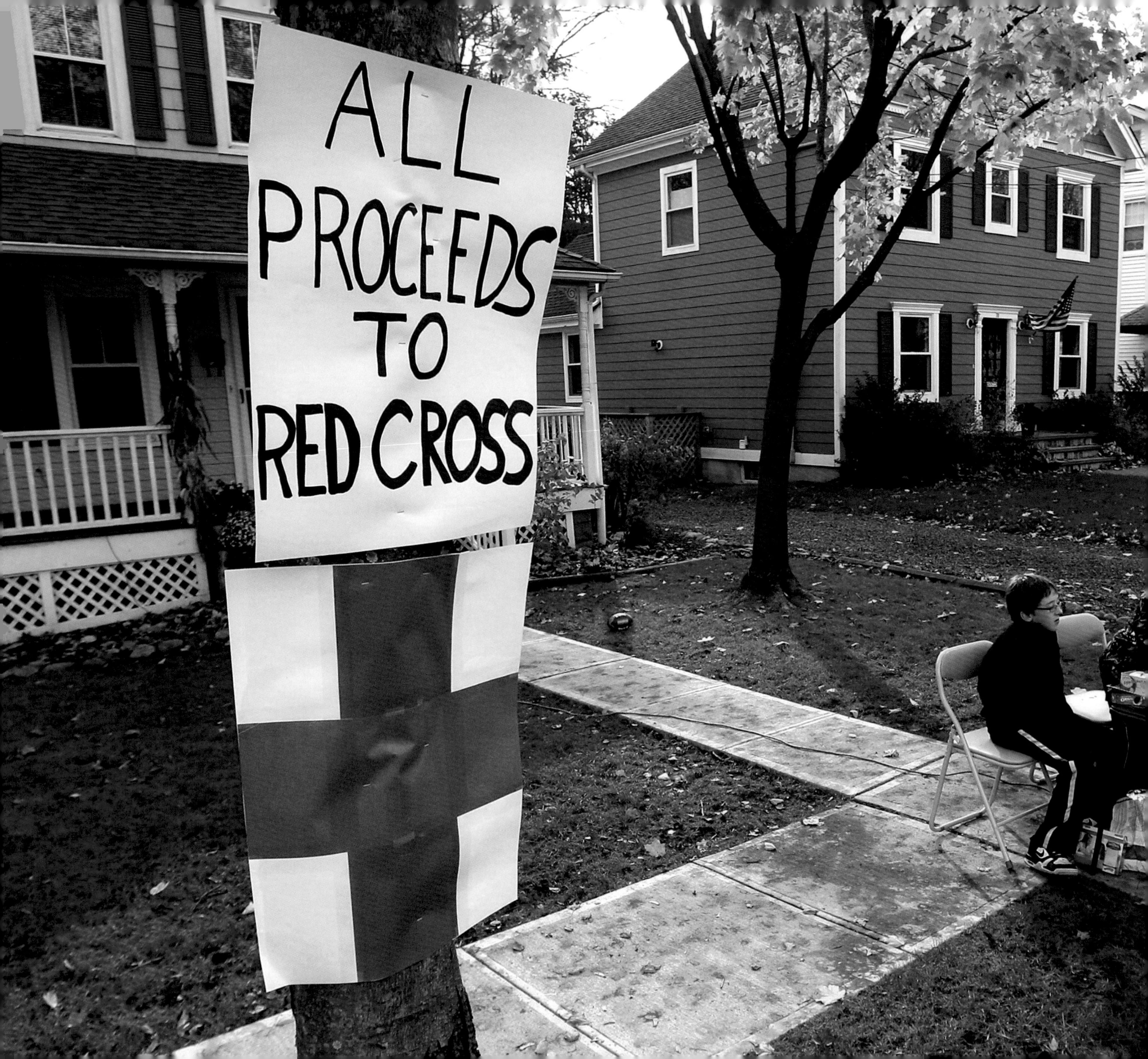
ALL
PROCEEDS
TO
RED CROSS

CHAPTER 7

Heroes of Sandy

C ops, firefighters, linemen, soldiers, doctors, nurses and EMTs played an invaluable role in guiding our communities through superstorm Sandy, and in managing the gritty weeks and months that followed. But heroes also emerged in all walks of life – from among neighbors and students, merchants and out-of-state volunteers—growing in number until it was hard to tell who was helping and who was being helped.

Nov. 1 — 9-year-old Hannah Leroux makes a donation to Nick Meyer (11) and Jack Konrad (8) who are collecting proceeds for the Red Cross on Hedges Avenue in Chatham. PHOTO BY BOB KARP

Nov. 7 — At right, a utility crew from Indian River, Mich., works on power lines in heavy, wet snow in Neptune. PHOTO BY TOM SPADER

Oct. 30 — Stafford Fire Dept workers try to locate Beach Haven West residents who want rides out of the flooded area. They had worked through the night getting people out of the flooded lagoon homes. The rescuers were at intersection of Morris and Walter boulevards.
PHOTO BY PETER ACKERMAN

Dec. 1 — Debbie Thompson, Helen Seiser and Louise Quist, all of Lacey, work to organize donations at Lacy United Methodist Church, where volunteers also prepared and served breakfast to Sandy Victims. PHOTO BY PETER ACKERMAN

Nov. 3 — At left, Highlands Police Chief Joseph Blewett, discusses the recovery effort from superstorm Sandy at a town hall meeting at the Highlands Elementary School. PHOTO BY ROBERT WARD

Dec. 25 — At top, Cathleen Keller of Toms River gives New Jersey State Trooper Chris Herman a hot dinner at a his post on Route 35 near Lavalette on Christmas Day in part of Restore the Shore: 1st Responders Christmas 2012. PHOTO BY TANYA BREEN

Dec. 25 — Above, Matt Rotonda of Toms River delivers dinners to Toms River Police Cpl. Sean McHugh at the command post located in the A&P parking lot in Ortley Beach on Christmas Day. PHOTO BY TANYA BREEN

Dec. 27 — Jon Simms of Winfield, a volunteer with U-Hungry Too, prepares Beef Stroganoff at VFW post 2179 in Middletown for Sandy victims.

PHOTO BY MARY FRANK

Dec. 27 — A volunteer at U-Hungry Too prepares peanut butter and jelly sandwiches.

PHOTO BY MARY FRANK

Dec. 27 — California volunteers with U-Hungry Too, Leslie Miller, 27, left, of San Diego and Brennan Crawford, 22, of Anaheim, announce the arrival of food at a condominium complex in Highlands. PHOTO BY MARY FRANK

Dec. 27 — U-Hungry Too volunteer Mike Robins, of Tucson, Ariz. chooses spices to use while preparing warm meals that will be distributed to the hungry.

PHOTO BY MARY FRANK

Nov. 4 — At left, Korinne Petrillo-Klug of Denville, Deputy Director of the Morris County Animal Response Team, with her English Bulldog, Tucker, at a 'Pop-Up Shelter' housing displaced homeowners and their pets at the Mennen Arena.

PHOTO BY BOB KARP

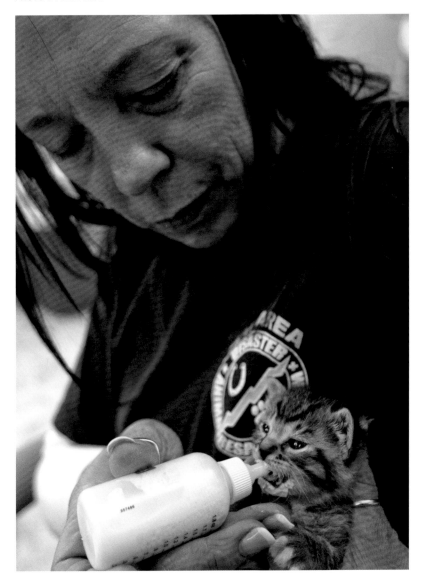

Nov. 8 — Billie Lambert of St. Petersburg, Fla., a volunteer with the Humane Society, feeds a three-week-old kitten separated from its mother, at a temporary emergency animal shelter on Collinstown Road in Barnegat.

PHOTO BY PETER ACKERMAN

Nov. 4 — At left, Morristown police Detective Keith Hudson directs cars lining up for gas on Pine Street.
PHOTO BY BOB KARP

Nov. 5 — Governor Chris Christie shakes hands with Joe Bellotti, lieutenant with the Keansburg Volunteer Fire Department, during visit to the Bolger Middle School in Keansburg.
PHOTO BY ROBERT WARD

Nov. 10 — Rutgers University gymnasts Nicole Romano (left) and Alyssa Straub collect donations for the American Red Cross at the Army-Rutgers football game. MARK R. SULLIVAN

Dec. 5 — At left, Firefighteres battle a blaze in Manasquan in a neighborhood already damaged by superstorm Sandy. PHOTO BY TOM SPADER

Nov. 1 — The staff at the Hunterdon County Complex in Raritan Township, where storm victims found shelter, and a place to charge phones and use the Internet. PHOTO BY KATHY JOHNSON

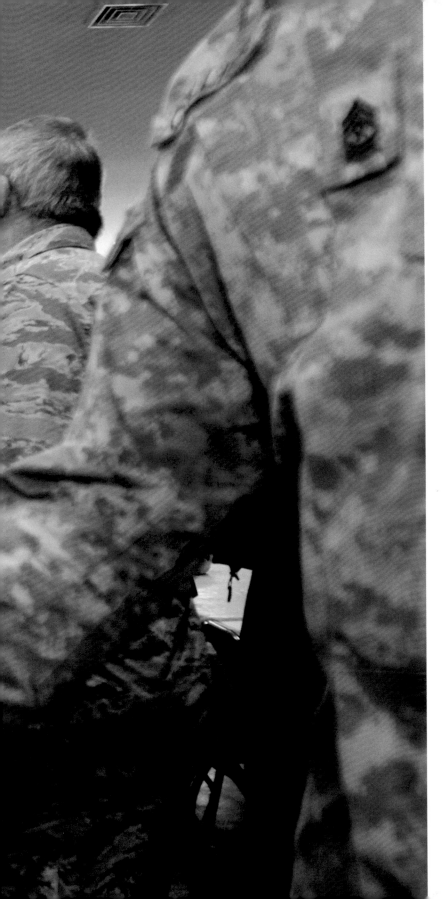

Nov. 7 — At left, Governor Chris Christie thanks National Guardsmen for their service during an appearance in Long Branch.

PHOTO BY THOMAS P. COSTELLO

Oct. 30 — Edison firefighters battle an early-morning house fire on Heathcote Avenue.

PHOTO BY JASON TOWLEN

Dec. 18 — NJ DOT commissioner James Simpson (left) and Andrew Tunnard, Director of Operations Support for DOT, survey homes along Route 35 in Brick. PHOTO BY BOB BIELK

Oct. 30 — Union Beach patrolmen Shawn Gilkison and Robert Harriott retrieve essentials from Harriott's sister's Prospect Avenue home, which was severely damaged in Sandy. PHOTO BY TANYA BREEN

Nov. 4 — Volunteer Bill Shine hands a bottle
of water to his wife Cheryl as they work to
redistribute donated food. The South Plainfield
P.A.L. organized a relief station at the Senior
Citizens Center for residents still in need of power,
food and other supplies. PHOTO BY AUGUSTO F. MENEZES

Nov. 18 — New Jersey Lt. Gov. Kim Guadagno, left, and Vice President Joe Biden — shaking hands with Zach Margaretta — during a vist to the Seaside Heights Firehouse.

PHOTO BY THOMAS P. COSTELLO

Nov. 9 — Governor Chris Christie shakes hands
with Spring Lake Police Chief Ed Kerr during a
visit to the Spring Lake pavilion on the boardwalk.

PHOTO BY THOMAS P. COSTELLO

Nov. 9 — Power crews work on the lines at Route 36 and River Street in Sea Bright.
PHOTO BY THOMAS P. COSTELLO

Nov. 5 — Ray Schucht of Brick helps unload food, water and clothing from Pittsburgh at the First Presbyterian Church in Manasquan.
PHOTO BY TOM SPADER

Nov. 20 — Bags of food await distribution at the Aldersgate United Methodist Church in East Brunswick. PHOTO BY MARK R. SULLIVAN

Oct. 30 — At left, a Perth Amboy firefighter walks up Gordon Street near the badly damaged waterfront. PHOTO BY JASON TOWLEN

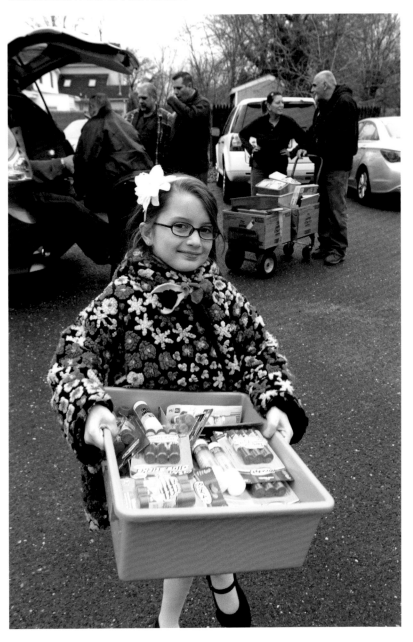

Dec. 17 — Rylie Wallace, 8, of North Kingstown, R.I., unloads donations she collected for Union Beach Memorial School students at their temporary location St. Catherine's School.
PHOTO BY TANYA BREEN

CHAPTER 8

Flood...then fire

A little over three months after the Seaside Heights Boardwalk was rebuilt for the summer season, its southern end was incinerated by fire. On the wind-swept afternoon of September 12, 2013, a small fire started around a frozen custard stand in neighboring Seaside Park's boardwalk.

The fire quickly raced north, engulfing the FunTown Pier, hard-hit by Sandy. More than 60 other businesses, booths, eateries and bars were also destroyed. By nightfall, five boardwalk blocks in two towns were reduced to ash, yet no serious injuries were reported. It was almost the same area that caught fire in 1955.

The new refrain for weary residents: We will rebuild. Again.

Sept. 12 — Fire engulfs the boardwalks in Seaside Park and Seaside Heights. PHOTO BY BOB BIELK

PREVIOUS PAGE
Sept. 12 — An aerial view of the Seaside Park Boardwalk fire in the late afternoon.
PHOTO BY PETER ACKERMAN

Sept. 12 — Flames rip through the Street Corner store sign along the Seaside Park Boardwalk. PHOTO BY THOMAS P. COSTELLO

Sept. 12 — Firefighters stand in ankle-deep water along Ocean Avenue as they try to bring the boardwalk fire under control.
PHOTO BY ROBERT WARD

Sept. 12 — **Firefighters on ladder trucks attempt to douse the fire with water pumped from the bay.** PHOTO BY BOB BIELK

PHOTO BY DOUG HOOD

PHOTO BY ROBERT WARD

Sept. 12 — Flames quickly engulf a beachfront building on the FunTown Pier in Seaside Park. PHOTO BY THOMAS P. COSTELLO

Sept. 12 — An aerial view of the Seaside Park Boardwalk.
PHOTO PETER ACKERMAN

Sept. 13 — The charred remains of five blocks of boardwalk in Seaside Park and Seaside Heights. The Lincoln Avenue fire trench, where the boardwalk was cut in two, is seen in the foreground.

PHOTO BY BOB BIELK

Sept. 13 — The sign for the FunTown Pier is one of the few remaining structures left standing after the fire.
PHOTO BY TOM SPADER

Sept. 13 — A firefighter on the scene at the Seaside Park Boardwalk the day after the fire. PHOTO BY TOM SPADER

Sept. 13 — At right, twisted metal is all that stands at the FunTown Pier the day after the fire. PHOTO BY TOM SPADER

Sept. 13 — Brian Gabriel, the chief fire coordinator for Ocean County, gives the media a quick tour the day after the fire. PHOTO BY TOM SPADER

Sept. 13 — Brian Gabriel, the chief fire coordinator for Ocean County, shows the 70-foot wide trench that was cut across the boardwalk in Seaside Heights to stop the fire from spreading north.
PHOTO BY TOM SPADER

Sept. 13 — A welcome sign outside the FunTown Pier.
PHOTO BY TOM SPADER

Sept. 13 — A utility worker examines power transformers that fell during the fire. PHOTO BY TOM SPADER

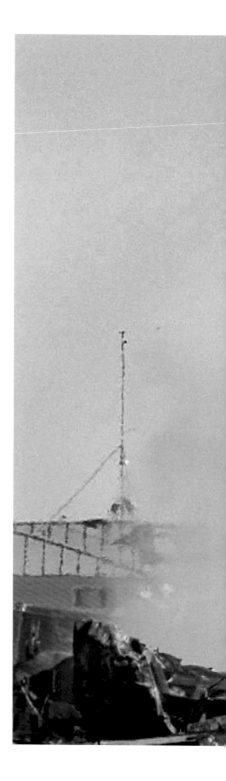

Sept. 14 — At right, two days after the fire, smoke still rises from the rubble near the Free Willy child's ride. PHOTO BY PETER ACKERMAN

Sept. 13 — Firefighters had to tear up the boardwalk at Lincoln Avenue in Seaside Heights to stop the spread of the fire. Without wood for fuel, the fire burned itself out. PHOTO BY TOM SPADER

Sept. 13 — Angie Lombardi, the owner of Angie's Alley on the Boardwalk, a business lost in the fire, is shocked when she sees the ruins a day after the fire. PHOTO BY TOM SPADER

Sept. 13 — Joe Maruca, manager of the family-owned Maruca's Pizza that was destroyed in the fire, looks over the wreckage. PHOTO BY TOM SPADER

Sept. 13 — A day after the fire is contained, Brian Gabriel, the chief fire coordinator for Ocean County, talks to media. PHOTO BY TOM SPADER

Sept. 13 — Gov. Chris Christie arrives at the fire scene the day after it was contained. PHOTO BY TOM SPADER

Sept. 13 — The melted skeleton of an amusement ride at the
FunTown Pier in Seaside Park. PHOTO BY TOM SPADER

Sept. 16 — Investigators examine the debris for clues to the cause of the fire. Authorities determined the blaze was accidental, sparked by 1970s wiring that had corroded beneath the Seaside Park Boardwalk. PHOTO BY THOMAS P. COSTELLO

June 9, 1955

Fifty-eight years before the 2013 fire, nearly the same section of boardwalk burned along Seaside Heights and Seaside Park.

PHOTOS FROM THE TERRY GROFFIE COLLECTION/COURTESY SEASIDE HEIGHTS VOLUNTEER FIRE COMPANY MUSEUM

PHOTOS FROM THE TERRY GROFFIE COLLECTION/COURTESY SEASIDE HEIGHTS VOLUNTEER FIRE COMPANY MUSEUM

'Unthinkable'

Sandy couldn't take the Seaside Park Boardwalk in 2012. But the 2013 fire did. These pages from the Asbury Park Press tell the story through photographs in the days after the fire. Gov. Chris Christie summed up the one-two punch against the towns with a single word: "Unthinkable."

Behind the headlines

For three groups of New Jersey Press Media staffers — reporters, designers and web producers — covering superstorm Sandy was the challenge of a lifetime.

In the field, reporters headed to the Shore as residents headed away, battening down in places from which they could witness the full fury of the storm. Even as lights blinked out and basements flooded in their own homes, they stayed on the job, acting as the eyes and ears for a region under siege.

As readers and visitors to APP.com would testify, the information generated by the reporting team was a lifeline.

When the fate of their houses and loved ones was still unknown, staying connected provided a context for hope.

Back in our Design Studio, designers and graphic artists kept up with a torrent of words and images, presenting them in innovative and effective ways.

And our web producers worked around the clock, posting content, sending thousands of tweets and text alerts, communicating with audiences on Facebook, answering questions, and sharing contributed news and photos.

THE PHOTOGRAPHY & VIDEO TEAM

PETER ACKERMAN "I captured images of Sandy's destruction from the air and on foot … from a roller coaster flung into the sea to damaged – and missing – houses. Happily, I also photographed residents beginning to put their lives back together and neighbors helping neighbors, which illuminated better days ahead."

MAGGIE BASSETT "I was proud and honored to work with such a dedicated staff during the tough and busy weeks of covering Sandy. It reminded me that this is my passion; this is why I choose this career. The results were amazing."

BOB BIELK "At first, I thought Sandy would be like all the others. No way. I will always remember the videos I shot the night that Sandy hit, with the wind howling, the transformers sparking overhead and the waves crashing on the shorelines of Keyport, Belmar and Asbury Park. This was not a storm like all the others. It was a storm your grandchildren will ask you about."

JIM CONNOLLY began his professional career in 1980. In 1982, he became a staff photographer at the Asbury Park Press, where he went on to serve as Chief Photographer and Photo Assignment Editor. He is Multimedia Editor for New Jersey Press Media, which comprises the Asbury Park Press, Home News Tribune, Courier News and Daily Record.

I'VE COVERED MANY STORMS over the years, including the nor'easter of 1992, which I thought would be the most devastating. Unfortunately I was wrong.

As Sandy grew into a superstorm, I began to worry – not about producing amazing images in difficult circumstances, but for the photo team's safety. Almost all of us lived in Sandy's projected bulls-eye.

Another problem: the simultaneous loss of power and destruction of cell towers, which turned simple communication into a nightmare – not to mention the transmission of images and videos.

But the quality of work from our staff – as they all juggled personal emergencies at home – was the best I've seen during three decades in this business. And I am honored to be a part of this team as we tell the story of rebirth at the Jersey Shore.

KATHY JOHNSON "Superstorm Sandy had the most widespread impact of any storm I have covered. Damage from enormous downed trees, not to mention power outages, were everywhere. In documenting the storm's damage to property and people, I was impressed by the positive spirit and helpful nature of the people I came across. It was great to be able to send photos and video clips from the field, as well as tweet news photos live from the hardest-hit areas."

ROBERT KARP "After covering Hurricane Irene I thought it would be easier to photograph Sandy. But where Irene brought floods, Sandy brought downed trees, power lines and gas shortages. It was a different challenge covering this disaster, but it's why I wanted to be a photojournalist. The worse the elements, the harder you want to do a great job bringing back strong images for your readers.

AUGUSTO MENEZES "Before Sandy, we've had many communities suffering catastrophic flooding in our coverage area. Like those other times, Sandy again brought me face-to-face with people who had lost everything. If I were in their shoes, with mouths to feed, I don't know what I would do."

TANYA BREEN "I can remember standing, almost frozen in time, on the corner of Brook Avenue and Union Avenue in Union Beach the morning after Sandy hit. A block of homes was flattened; there was nothing intact but cement staircases that once lead to a front door. Even when surrounded by such devastation, I could feel the town's unity, strength, perseverance and selflessness. I was honored to be their voice through pictures."

THOMAS P. COSTELLO "I grew up along the Jersey Shore and spent many summers working on the Seaside Heights boardwalk. Many places that I grew up with were wiped away in one night. It the wake of Sandy, it has been encouraging to see people smile as they remember the Jersey Shore that was, and their dreams for the stronger one that will come."

MARY FRANK "No one could have anticipated the wrath Sandy would bring to our beloved Jersey Shore. Everywhere you turned was destruction, but I was impressed with the resilience of residents and the kindness of volunteers, some of them strangers, who opened their arms and homes to help those in need. I'm grateful to Sandy victims who, in spite of all their troubles, were kind enough to let us into their homes to tell their story."

DOUG HOOD Superstorm Sandy and her aftermath has, by far, had the most impact on me personally. My home was flooded, so dealing with my personal situation – as well as covering other peoples' stories – has been interesting to say the least. I simply try to take it day by day and learn from others I talk to while on the job. It looks like a long road ahead for many of us. Good luck!"

THOMAS SPADER "After 25 years of covering the news, when Sandy hit I became the news. We lost the first floor of our home in Point Pleasant Beach and a car, forcing me to cover Sandy's aftermath on foot in my hometown. Like many I will never be same, taking nothing for granted, but also seeing the compassion and good in the people around us."

MARK SULLIVAN "Being a lifelong resident of the Jersey Shore, it broke my heart to photograph the devastation that occurred during Super Storm Sandy. I hope and pray that the victims of the storm stay Jersey Strong and come back better than ever."

JASON TOWLEN "Covering Superstorm Sandy has been a challenging and emotional experience. Sandy brought out the best in New Jersey. As devastating as the storm was, documenting the recovery has been truly inspirational."

ROBERT WARD "Covering Sandy and the aftermath, I am amazed at not only the storm's destruction but the resiliency of the people involved. I was also moved by the generosity and compassion shown to the victims by strangers. It restored my faith in humanity."

Weathering the storm together

We were there with you when Sandy began her destructive path up the Shore.

We were there with you when the lights went out, and you awoke to find your community changed forever.

And because we are connected by 133 years of history, we will be there with you as the Shore rebuilds. This time, the rebuilding is not just from superstorm Sandy, but from the ravages of a devastating fire in Seaside Park. The fire's fury didn't douse the region's commitment to rebuild, but rather, it strengthened it.

The staff at APP.com and the Asbury Park Press is committed to the communities we serve.

Sandy shook our region, but she never shook out commitment to you. When the lights went out on the Jersey Shore, and later, when word traveled that a raging fire was burning out of control in Seaside Park, you turned to APP.com and the Asbury Park Press to stay connected.

Thank you!

We will always remain committed to delivering quality local news. After all, we share a commitment that has enabled us to weather many disasters – together.

HOLLIS R. TOWNS
VP/NEWS